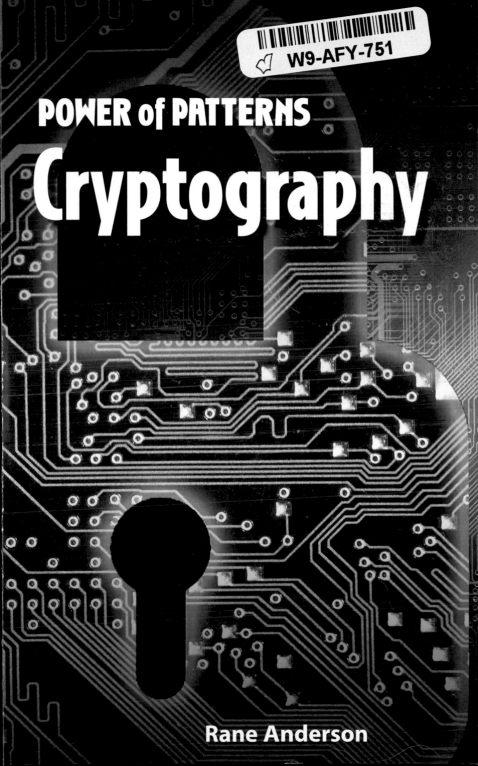

POWER of PATTERNS
Cryptography

Rane Anderson

Consultants

Timothy Rasinski, Ph.D.
Kent State University

Lori Oczkus, M.A.
Literacy Consultant

Publishing Credits

Rachelle Cracchiolo, M.S.Ed., *Publisher*
Conni Medina, M.A.Ed., *Managing Editor*
Dona Herweck Rice, *Series Developer*
Emily R. Smith, M.A.Ed., *Content Director*
Stephanie Bernard/Noelle Cristea, M.A.Ed., *Editors*
Robin Erickson, *Senior Graphic Designer*

The TIME logo is a registered trademark of TIME Inc. Used under license.

Image Credits: p.5 Courtesy of Laura W. Petix; p.6 Sergiy Tryapitsyn/ Alamy Stock Photo; p.8 Everett Collection/Newscom; p.11 Georgios Kollidas/Dreamstime.com; p.16 Archive Image/Alamy Stock Photo; p.34 dpa picture alliance/Alamy Stock Photo; p.35 and back cover Luringen/Wikimedia Commons License: Creative Commons BY-SA 3.0/ https://goo.gl/3KiQ3W; p.42 Louis Berk/Alamy Stock Photo; all other images from iStock and/or Shutterstock.

Note: The answers to the mathematical problems posed throughout the book are provided on page 48.

Library of Congress Cataloging-in-Publication Data

Names: Anderson, Rane.
Title: Cryptography / Rane Anderson.
Description: Huntington Beach, CA : Teacher Created Materials, [2017] | Series: Power of patterns | Includes index.
Identifiers: LCCN 2016047684 (print) | LCCN 2016048864 (ebook) | ISBN 9781493836246 (pbk.) | ISBN 9781480757288 (eBook)
Subjects: LCSH: Cryptography--Juvenile literature. | Ciphers--Juvenile literature.
Classification: LCC Z103.3 .A58 2017 (print) | LCC Z103.3 (ebook) | DDC 652/.8--dc23
LC record available at https://lccn.loc.gov/2016047684

Teacher Created Materials

5301 Oceanus Drive
Huntington Beach, CA 92649-1030
http://www.tcmpub.com

ISBN 978-1-4938-3624-6

Table of Contents

Mysterious Messages

Imagine you're standing in an old, quiet graveyard in England. Every dreary headstone looks the same—except one. The headstone displays the usual name and date but also has several strange, unreadable symbols carved into the stone. What could they mean?

This true-life mystery from the nineteenth century stumped everyone who saw the odd progression of symbols. It caught the attention of reporters and authors, mystifying many. Some people said the symbols were Greek letters. Others thought they might be Hebrew letters. But the truth was that only a select group, the **Freemasons**, could understand the inscription.

In the eighteenth century, Freemasons used the same symbols to create **cryptographs**, or coded messages. Afraid of **persecution** for their beliefs, they disguised their potentially dangerous ideas and records in secret **ciphers**. But they weren't the only ones who did this. Throughout history, other clever people like the Freemasons have found creative ways to communicate in secret. By using numbers, letters, and symbols to make ciphers, they sent and received messages nobody else could understand.

Deadly Decoding

In 1586, Mary, Queen of Scots, used a cipher to conceal a sinister scheme to kill her cousin Queen Elizabeth I of England. But soon after, her coded letters fell into the wrong hands. A spymaster **decrypted** the message that proved Mary's guilt, and the English queen beheaded Mary for treason.

Here lies deposited the Body of

James Leeson

Cabinet Noir

In the 1590s, King Henry IV of France opened the *Cabinet Noir*, which translates to the *Black Chamber*. His workers opened, read, and resealed letters written by his subjects. When people figured out how the king knew everyone's secrets, they began to write their letters in code. The king then had his workers decrypt coded messages, and the *Cabinet Noir* became the first unofficial cipher bureau.

Decrypting Cryptography

These days, people send messages through texts, emails, or social media apps. Virtual messages travel from sender to receiver in a matter of seconds. But not that long ago, a letter could only be delivered by hand, sometimes traveling for months before reaching the receiver.

These messages sometimes had to cross great physical obstacles, such as battle lines or oceans. Kings, commanders, and soldiers often wrote letters that held highly confidential information. Their letters might have contained reports about enemy defenses, identities of spies, or orders to move or attack. And each message faced high risk of **interception**.

Intercepted messages had the power to change the course of a war, put thousands of lives at risk, or even lead to the dethroning of a king or a queen. A coded message, on the other hand, could protect state secrets. If the message happened to fall into enemy hands, no one could read it without the **key**. Cryptography—the science of writing messages with a secret meaning—solved the problem of interception.

Cryptography Today

Today, cryptography still protects state secrets. Since the **advent** of personal computers and the World Wide Web, cryptography plays a daily part in the average person's life. It is used in computer programs, Internet traffic, cell phones, and other electronic devices. People depend on and benefit from cryptography.

Cipher Styles

Cryptographs can be divided into two types: transposition and substitution. Transposition focuses on scrambling letters into a new order. For example, *apple* becomes *eplap*. Substitution switches one letter for a different letter, number, or symbol, such as the *a* in *apple* becoming @. Though different in many ways, both cipher styles require the sender *and* the receiver to know the key and the method of decrypting—the procedure that unscrambles the message.

THINK LINK

◎ What ways can you think of to transpose letters in a written message?

◎ How might one cipher style be more beneficial than the other?

◎ What problems might occur if the receiver of a cipher does not know which method of decryption to use?

Navajo Code Talkers

During World War II, the U.S. Marines used the Navajo language to communicate over the radio. Very few non-Navajos knew the language, which made it a secure method of communication. For example, the English letter *A* was represented by the English word "ant." Then, that would be translated into *wol-la-chee* in the Navajo language.

Codes

Ladies and gentleman, Elvis has left the building! If you have ever watched a spy movie, you've most likely heard the use of a code word or phrase. Unlike ciphers, which operate on syntax, or symbols, codes generally deal with semantics, or the meaning of words and phrases. For example, a phrase such as "Elvis has left the building!" might be code for "Special forces have completed their mission and are coming home!" A code word or phrase more than likely has a literal meaning as well, but people "in the know" will also understand that its second, hidden meaning is the one worth knowing. Don't forget, for codes to work, both the sender and receiver need a copy of the same codebook to create and interpret messages.

Ciphers

Unlike codes, where each word or message is replaced with another word or symbol, mathematics and patterns play large roles in creating ciphers. In a cipher, every letter in a message is replaced. Cipher makers use special procedures to jumble up plaintext—the letters that make up a correspondence prior to **encryption**—with different letters, words, numbers, or symbols. These procedures vary in difficulty. Can you identify the procedure used to create this simple cipher?

rekaerbedoc emosewa na ma i

You might have figured out that the plaintext reads, *I am an awesome codebreaker*. The procedure for this cipher included only one step: to write the message backwards.

A two-step procedure might look a little different. Can you figure out the difference?

reka erbe docemo sew ana mai

In the second step of this cipher, the letters are separated at different intervals.

These are simple examples, but ciphers today rely on complex mathematics to decrypt and encrypt—to convert into a scrambled message.

Morse Code

Beep, beep, beeeeeeeeep. Morse code uses a series of dots and dashes that convert into electric signals to transmit messages over telegraphs. Skilled listeners pick up the clicks or beeps over telegraphs and convert the sounds back into English letters.

MORSE CODE

A .- B -... C -.-. D -.. E . F ..-.
G --. H .... I .. J .--- K -.- L .-..
M -- N -. O --- P .--. Q --.- R .-.
S ... T - U ..- V ...- W .--
X -..- Y -.-- Z --..

Laws of Cryptography

How would you like to devise a secret code or cipher of your own? Dutch author and **cryptographer** from the nineteenth century, Auguste Kerckhoffs, would ask you to keep the following considerations in mind:

- Above all, your code or cipher should be unbreakable.

- If an enemy can identify the basic procedure, or algorithm, you're using, it doesn't mean the cipher is inadequate. As long as the key to the cipher stays secret, the secret message is safe.

- The key should be easy to remember and easy to modify.

- The ciphertext, which is what you're left with after the encryption process, should be easy to deliver to the receiver.

- If you're using some kind of cipher device, the device should be easy to use and transport.

- Lastly, challenge a friend to break the algorithm. If it's well built, he or she won't discover the hidden message unless you provide the key.

Although Kerckhoffs wrote these guidelines in the 1800s, the concepts are still relevant today. However, in the age of technology, creating ciphers has become more complex. With the use of computers, it is now much easier to break algorithms. Therefore, there's always an urgency to develop new ones.

Finding Fatal Flaws

Kerckhoffs also says it's better to go public with an algorithm and let the world try to break it. Gifted **cryptanalysts** will put it to the test, and then the designer will know whether it's unbreakable. A cryptographer who doesn't do this will never know if his or her algorithm has a fatal flaw.

Hidden in Plain Sight

Next time you get a letter in the mail, take a closer look. Is it really just a normal letter, or does it possibly contain a secret message? Letters are common places for secret messages. As an alternative to codes and ciphers, **steganography** is a way to hide messages in plain sight. It has its advantages. For example, a slip of paper covered in strange symbols or chunks of jumbled letters might draw unwanted attention. But when a message is hidden within another message, no one would know or even suspect that it's there.

Before the digital age, people had to find clever ways to hide messages. They would use secret compartments, invisible ink, tiny markings on book pages, and word or spacing patterns. Now in the twenty-first century, encoders use high-tech ways to disguise messages in plain sight. In fact, embedding, or hiding, a secret message in plain sight, such as in a digital file, is so effective that it's undetectable to the human eye or ear. Secret messages can lurk in many forms of **cover text**, such as images, audio files, videos, emails, or web pages. The sky is the limit.

Butterfly Wings

In the late 1800s, a British spy would sit outside enemy forts posing as a butterfly collector. In his butterfly wings sketches, he disguised vital military intelligence, such as the structure of the fort and the number and positions of weapons.

d fashioned / all nat

Message Masks

During the American Revolution, spies used Cardan Grilles to unmask secret messages in otherwise innocent letters. The grille, made from thick paper or metal, had rectangles cut out of it in seemingly random positions. Placing the grille over the right correspondence would reveal letters or words that combined to reveal a secret message. The one below reads, "conspiracy."

C

D

N

S

P

I

A C

Y

liquid / citrate / vitamin D / 6 varieties

Image Files

Picture files on computers contain large numbers of dots called *pixels*. Each pixel has a position and color linked with it. Advanced software tools can use the patterns detected within the image file and subtly alter the properties of certain pixels. The result is a secret message hidden within the image that doesn't look different from the original, unaltered one.

Stegotext

If an encoder wants to ensure a message is very secure within a covertext, he or she will encrypt it first. Then, the decoder will need to know how the message, known as **stegotext**, is hidden, as well as how to decrypt it.

If you zoom in on the image, you can see each pixel.

Audio Files

An audio file is filled with dips and spikes. This can especially be seen in music since it includes many instruments and vocals. Software tools can alter some of the spikes or add new ones to encrypt a piece of audio. Most of the time, the average person will not be able to detect the encryption. A codebreaker has to run the encrypted file back through the special software on his or her computer to extract the hidden message.

Secret Message Songs

Some songs reveal secret messages in their lyrics when played backwards. This type of encryption is called *reverse speech*, and it is believed that many artists have used the technique to intentionally insert messages into their songs.

MIS-X

In 1942 during WWII, a classified program known as Military Intelligence Service-X (MIS-X) trained pilots to become code users, or CUs. The training prepared them to send secret messages. If these pilots were captured, they would become spies in the prisoner of war (POW) camps and send intelligence messages hidden in ordinary letters.

CUs used a simple pattern that formed sentences from different words found throughout a letter. To do this, all incoming letters from POW camps were screened for the names of known CUs in case the letters were coded. If the date at the top of the letter was written in numerals, the person screening the mail knew it was coded and gave it to a cryptanalyst to decrypt. The decrypted message was passed along through the chain of command, then the original letter was resealed and mailed.

Using this method, U.S. intelligence officers were able to communicate with nearly every POW camp through the end of WWII. The Germans never discovered the scheme; only a select group of people even knew of its existence. The information has been recently **declassified**.

The MIS-X Algorithm

1. CUs wrote dates at the tops of the letters in numerals, such as 3/7/42, to let MIS-X know that they were coded letters.

2. Multiplying the numbers of letters in the first two words told how many code words were in the letter. For example, *how* (3 letters) x *good* (4 letters) = 12 code words.

3. To find the code words, officers began at the second sentence and counted five words, then six words, then five words, until all the code words were extracted. Then the message could be unscrambled, as shown below.

3/7/42

How good to hear from you again.

Just returned from the station where we unloaded a supply train all morning. I plumb near sprained my back lugging all the crates of food to camp. There's a sergeant here named North who lives just outside of Salinas! Small world. His Uncle Miles works in the salvage factory where Aunt Clarice worked. For two years I've been craving ground sausage or almost any meat under the sun. Given nothing but powdered eggs and turnips it's a wonder we've survived this camp.

station train near the camp North of Miles factory two ground under

Unscrambled message:
Underground factory two miles north of camp near the train station

Transposition Ciphers

Have you ever unscrambled a word puzzle for a school activity or perhaps just for fun? If you have, you've decrypted a secret message! Transposition ciphers use fairly straightforward algorithms (step-by-step instructions) that scramble plaintext in new and complex ways. Writing the plaintext *I am an awesome codebreaker* backwards demonstrates the simplest form of a transposition cipher. But keep in mind that they can get *much* more complicated.

The Rail Fence Hop

The rail fence cipher was a favorite among spies during the American Civil War. The cipher below uses a three-row key and looks like this:

R			F			E			H		
	A		L	E		C		C		P		E
		I			N			I				R

Here, the letters stagger down and up in a diagonal direction using three rows, or "fence rails." Taking the letters from the top, middle, and bottom rows produces the following ciphertext that would be sent to the recipient:

RFEHALECCPEINIR

Rail Fence Rules

1. The cipher key represents the number of rows in the grid (3).

2. The length of the plaintext must be equivalent to the number of columns in the grid (15).

Cipher Blast!

Can you break this rail fence cipher?

TLTRHEHLOSRETTELTEATSOGHNBLBINAU

(32 letters in plaintext)

Key = 4

1. Use graph paper to make a 32-column by 4-row grid.
2. Highlight the boxes in a diagonal down-and-up pattern beginning in the top left box.
3. Place the first letter in the top left corner, working across the row to fill in only the highlighted boxes.
4. Then, fill the second, third, and fourth rows successively.
5. Read the message!

Civil War generals reading a document

19

Route Cipher

Another spy favorite from the Civil War days, the route cipher transposes plaintext by selecting a specific route to follow within a grid. Let's encrypt the following plaintext: *Mission compromised.*

1. Create a grid that will fit the size of the plaintext message. The plaintext consists of 18 letters. That means the cipher requires at least a 6 x 3 grid, since that would have an exact area of 18, but it's okay if it's a little larger, too.

~~4 columns x 3 rows = 12 boxes~~	too small
~~4 columns x 4 rows = 16 boxes~~	too small
6 columns x 3 rows = 18 boxes	this works
4 columns x 5 rows = 20 boxes	this works, too

The grid can be constructed using several types of shapes, but it's less complicated to use a square or a rectangle.

2. Add the plaintext letters in a logical sequence, such as left to right. When you come to the last box in the row, move to the beginning of the next row.

3. If there are empty boxes, put a **null** inside each to fill it. Nulls can be any letter, but in this instance, the null is an X.

4. Select a route to follow to encrypt the plaintext message, such as an inward spiral moving counterclockwise, beginning in the bottom left corner as shown on page 21. The route can be anything that you want!

Grid with chosen route

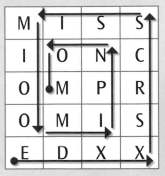

Reversing the Route

To reverse the cipher, the codebreaker must know the dimensions of the grid and the route in advance. Then, he or she can create a grid following those specifications and plug in the ciphertext using the same route to reveal the secret message.

Civil War Jumble

Civil War soldiers used a variation of the route cipher. Instead of transposing a message letter by letter, they would do it using whole words. The message "Attack at midnight on the colonel's orders" would instead say, "orders midnight on at attack the colonel's." Then they'd combine the cipher with a code to conceal the highly sensitive words like "attack" and "colonel."

Here's Another!

What are your options for a grid that needs to fit a plaintext message that consists of 36 letters?

Creating a Columnar Cipher

A columnar cipher closely resembles a route cipher, except it uses a **keyword** as a guide to rearrange plaintext letters. Let's encrypt the plaintext: *rendezvous at midnight*.

1. Select a keyword, and number its letters based on their order in the alphabet. In this example, our keyword is *cipher*.

keyword:	C	I	P	H	E	R
alphabet order:	1	4	5	3	2	6

2. Since the keyword contains six letters, the grid needs six columns. But how many rows does it require? The plaintext *Rendezvous at midnight* is 20 letters long, so the grid must contain six columns and have enough boxes for 20 plaintext letters.

~~6 columns x 3 rows = 18 boxes~~ R	O	U	N	I	X
6 columns x 4 rows = 24 boxes E	V	S	D	G	X
N	Z	A	I	H	X
D	E	T	M	T	X

3. Add plaintext to each column in a logical sequence. For this example, we have started in the top left box, moving down the first column and up the next. Don't forget to fill the empty boxes with nulls. Because the keyword has six letters, we must have six filled columns.

4. Rearrange the columns into alphabetical order, as determined by the keyword.

Before					
C	**I**	**P**	**H**	**E**	**R**
1	4	5	3	2	6
R	O	U	N	I	X
E	V	S	D	G	X
N	Z	A	I	H	X
D	E	T	M	T	X

After					
C	**E**	**H**	**I**	**P**	**R**
1	2	3	4	5	6
R	I	N	O	U	X
E	G	D	V	S	X
N	H	I	Z	A	X
D	T	M	E	T	X

5. In the fashion of a route cipher, select any route you wish to encrypt the plaintext. This one follows a zigzag route starting with R in the top left box.

C	**E**	**H**	**I**	**P**	**R**
1	2	3	4	5	6
R	I	N	O	U	X
E	G	D	V	S	X
N	H	I	Z	A	X
D	T	M	E	T	X

RINOUXXSVDGENHIZAXXTEMTD

Brute Force Attack

Old ciphers, such as rail fence ciphers and columnar ciphers, are no longer secure to use. Although they take some time to compute with pen and paper, they rely on simple arithmetic. Computers, though, are exceptionally fast at doing this. A computer can complete a brute force attack, trying every possible combination on these ciphers in a matter of seconds.

Substitution Ciphers

Ju$t 4or your in4ormation, ubtitution cipher$ switch out one plaintext letter for another letter, number, or symbol. These ciphers also use algorithms to encrypt or decrypt secret messages. But no matter how hard you try, merely rearranging letters or trying to unscramble them will not get you any closer to cracking them.

Caesar's Simple Cipher

As a Roman general, Julius Caesar often dispatched secret messages to his troops that used a unique algorithm where each letter of the alphabet was shifted over. In this example, by how many is each letter shifted over?

A	B	C	D	E	F	G	H	I	J	K	L	M	N	O	P	Q	R	S	T	U	V	W	X	Y	Z
X	Y	Z	A	B	C	D	E	F	G	H	I	J	K	L	M	N	O	P	Q	R	S	T	U	V	W

Counting Letters

Certain letters in the English language are used more frequently than others, such as the letter *E*. So an attacker can conduct a frequency count. He or she will look for the most commonly used letters in the message. Take a look at this quotation by Julius Caesar and the corresponding Caesar's ciphertext below it:

EXPERIENCE IS THE TEACHER OF ALL THINGS
HASHULHQFH LV WKH WHDFKHU RI DOO WKLQJV

Notice that the letter *H* occurs seven times within the ciphertext on page 24. That's much more than any other letter in the message. So the codebreaker can assume the ciphertext letter *H* represents the plaintext letter *E* because *E* is the most frequent letter in the English language. Keep going with the rest of the letters and pretty soon, the codebreaker will figure out the algorithm, and then it's game over!

STOP! THINK...

This chart shows a letter frequency analysis of the text on page 16.

- Several letters fall within a similar frequency range. How might this help or hinder a codebreaker?

- Do you think it was possible to crack Caesar's cipher before the invention of the frequency count? Why, or why not?

Letter	Count	Frequency
E	124	15.35
T	69	8.54
S	64	7.92
N	61	7.55
I	57	7.05
O	51	6.31
R	51	6.31
A	46	5.69
D	36	4.46
C	35	4.33
H	30	3.71
L	29	3.59
M	27	3.34
W	23	2.85
P	21	2.60
F	20	2.48
G	18	2.23
U	17	2.10
Y	12	1.49
V	6	0.74
B	4	0.50
X	4	0.50
K	3	0.37
J	0	0.00
Q	0	0.00
Z	0	0.00

Breaking Ciphers

Imagine you're at school and find a crumpled-up piece of paper on the ground. Opening the paper, you see it's filled with a scramble of letters: **zh duh dzhvrph**. It could be someone's sloppy chemistry notes. But on second thought, could this gibberish be ciphertext? Figuring out how to break the cipher will take time and might prove challenging, but thinking like a codebreaker will make it easier to decrypt the message.

Thinking Like a Codebreaker

Conduct a frequency count by finding the letter that appears the most. Assume the plaintext of the most frequent letter equals E.

zh duh dzhvrph

In this example, the ciphertext letter H appears most often, so substitute the ciphertext letter H with the plaintext letter E.

zE duE dzEvrpE

Now, identify the second and third most frequent ciphertext letters, and find their plaintext equivalents. (Hint: Using the Caesar cipher on page 24 as a reference might help these words take shape! When you're done cracking the code, check your answer on page 48.)

The Ultimate Challenge

The most challenging cipher in this book appears on the paper below. There are clues hidden in this chapter to help you solve it. Here's one to get you started: this cipher is *double trouble*.

ECFHXXKMQUMYIRDYFLLXTZ

Pattern Problems

Identifying patterns within a cipher can be advantageous, but at all costs, it is important to avoid obvious patterns in cipher creation. Avoiding them usually requires a lot of trial and error. If a part of a cipher appears too obvious, it's wise to start over and use a different algorithm.

Double Trouble

Using more than one algorithm to encrypt a message will help prevent obvious patterns. For example, try using the Vigenère cipher (more about that on page 30) and then transposing that ciphertext with a rail fence cipher. This requires a lot more work, and errors could still occur. However, with careful planning and close attention to detail, you'll have an uncrackable code in no time.

Civil War Trickery

"Rebel Rose" Greenhow made a habit of eavesdropping on Union officers during the Civil War. She then used a 26-symbol code to encrypt and safely convey Union secrets back to the Confederates. To conceal a message, she and other female spies would hide it in the hair of a tight bun so if caught, the cryptograph wouldn't be found.

Rose Greenhow and her daughter

Pigpen Cipher

Now is your chance to try your hand at a modern version of the cipher from that English headstone on page 5. The pigpen cipher, also known as the Freemason cipher, substitutes plaintext letters for symbols. Looking at it, it may seem impossible to figure out what the seemingly random symbols stand for, but they are just as vulnerable to a frequency count attack as the Caesar cipher. Look for patterns in the message in the box below, and try your hand at a frequency count. (Or use the key below the box.)

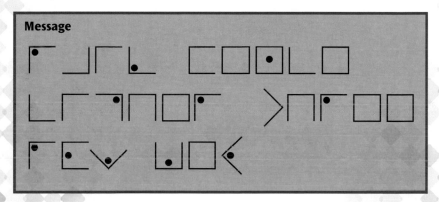

Message

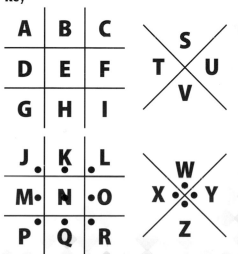

Key

The Unbreakable Vigenère Cipher

The French nicknamed the Vigenère cipher *le chiffre indéchiffrable,* which translates to "the indecipherable cipher." But ciphers can always be broken, and this one is no exception. Compared to most ciphers, the Vigenère is harder to break using only pen and paper methods since it uses a **polyalphabetic** algorithm. The Vigenère cipher introduces the use of an alphabet table called a tabula recta. In addition to a tabula recta, this algorithm uses a **keystream**, which when combined with plaintext, helps produce the ciphertext. Here is an example of a one-letter encryption using the tabula recta on page 31.

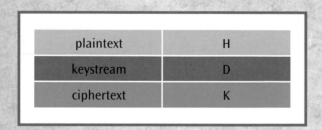

plaintext	H
keystream	D
ciphertext	K

Lincoln's Assassination

It is thought that John Wilkes Booth, one of many conspirators who plotted to assassinate Abraham Lincoln, had hidden a Vigenère cipher within his traveling trunk. It's believed the conspirators had planned the assassination by communicating through ciphers.

The box where they meet indicates the ciphertext letter.

Top row: Find the plaintext letter in this row.

Tabula Recta

	A	B	C	D	E	F	G	H	I	J	K	L	M	N	O	P	Q	R	S	T	U	V	W	X	Y	Z
A	A	B	C	D	E	F	G	H	I	J	K	L	M	N	O	P	Q	R	S	T	U	V	W	X	Y	Z
B	B	C	D	E	F	G	H	I	J	K	L	M	N	O	P	Q	R	S	T	U	V	W	X	Y	Z	A
C	C	D	E	F	G	H	I	J	K	L	M	N	O	P	Q	R	S	T	U	V	W	X	Y	Z	A	B
D	D	E	F	G	H	I	J	K	L	M	N	O	P	Q	R	S	T	U	V	W	X	Y	Z	A	B	C
E	E	F	G	H	I	J	K	L	M	N	O	P	Q	R	S	T	U	V	W	X	Y	Z	A	B	C	D
F	F	G	H	I	J	K	L	M	N	O	P	Q	R	S	T	U	V	W	X	Y	Z	A	B	C	D	E
G	G	H	I	J	K	L	M	N	O	P	Q	R	S	T	U	V	W	X	Y	Z	A	B	C	D	E	F
H	H	I	J	K	L	M	N	O	P	Q	R	S	T	U	V	W	X	Y	Z	A	B	C	D	E	F	G
I	I	J	K	L	M	N	O	P	Q	R	S	T	U	V	W	X	Y	Z	A	B	C	D	E	F	G	H
J	J	K	L	M	N	O	P	Q	R	S	T	U	V	W	X	Y	Z	A	B	C	D	E	F	G	H	I
K	K	L	M	N	O	P	Q	R	S	T	U	V	W	X	Y	Z	A	B	C	D	E	F	G	H	I	J
L	L	M	N	O	P	Q	R	S	T	U	V	W	X	Y	Z	A	B	C	D	E	F	G	H	I	J	K
M	M	N	O	P	Q	R	S	T	U	V	W	X	Y	Z	A	B	C	D	E	F	G	H	I	J	K	L
N	N	O	P	Q	R	S	T	U	V	W	X	Y	Z	A	B	C	D	E	F	G	H	I	J	K	L	M
O	O	P	Q	R	S	T	U	V	W	X	Y	Z	A	B	C	D	E	F	G	H	I	J	K	L	M	N
P	P	Q	R	S	T	U	V	W	X	Y	Z	A	B	C	D	E	F	G	H	I	J	K	L	M	N	O
Q	Q	R	S	T	U	V	W	X	Y	Z	A	B	C	D	E	F	G	H	I	J	K	L	M	N	O	P
R	R	S	T	U	V	W	X	Y	Z	A	B	C	D	E	F	G	H	I	J	K	L	M	N	O	P	Q
S	S	T	U	V	W	X	Y	Z	A	B	C	D	E	F	G	H	I	J	K	L	M	N	O	P	Q	R
T	T	U	V	W	X	Y	Z	A	B	C	D	E	F	G	H	I	J	K	L	M	N	O	P	Q	R	S
U	U	V	W	X	Y	Z	A	B	C	D	E	F	G	H	I	J	K	L	M	N	O	P	Q	R	S	T
V	V	W	X	Y	Z	A	B	C	D	E	F	G	H	I	J	K	L	M	N	O	P	Q	R	S	T	U
W	W	X	Y	Z	A	B	C	D	E	F	G	H	I	J	K	L	M	N	O	P	Q	R	S	T	U	V
X	X	Y	Z	A	B	C	D	E	F	G	H	I	J	K	L	M	N	O	P	Q	R	S	T	U	V	W
Y	Y	Z	A	B	C	D	E	F	G	H	I	J	K	L	M	N	O	P	Q	R	S	T	U	V	W	X
Z	Z	A	B	C	D	E	F	G	H	I	J	K	L	M	N	O	P	Q	R	S	T	U	V	W	X	Y

Left column: Find the keystream letter in this column.

Encrypting a Vigenère

Now, let's join the big leagues by encrypting a message using the Vigenère cipher. Use the plaintext: *decoding is fun*.

1. Create a three-row grid that has the same number of columns as the plaintext. For *decoding is fun*, you'd use 13 columns.

2. Select a keystream, such as *i love ciphers*. A keystream does not need to be the same length as the plaintext. In this case, it's one letter shorter, so you start it over.

plaintext	d	e	c	o	d	i	n	g	i	s	f	u	n
keystream	i	l	o	v	e	c	i	p	h	e	r	s	i
ciphertext													

3. Now, use the tabula recta on page 33 to fill in the ciphertext row. Find the first plaintext letter on the top row of the table. Follow the column straight down until you see the corresponding keystream letter in the far left column. The letter you land on is the ciphertext letter. Write that letter in the table. For example, the first ciphertext letter for this encryption is **L**.

4. Repeat Step 3 until each plaintext letter has been encrypted.

plaintext	d	e	c	o	d	i	n	g	i	s	f	u	n
keystream	i	l	o	v	e	c	i	p	h	e	r	s	i
ciphertext	**L**	**P**	**Q**	**J**	**H**	**K**	**V**	**V**	**P**	**W**	**W**	**M**	**V**

5. This is the ciphertext to send the recipient:
   LPQJHKVVPWWMV

	A	B	C	D	E	F	G	H	I	J	K	L	M	N	O	P	Q	R	S	T	U	V	W	X	Y	Z
A	A	B	C	D	E	F	G	H	I	J	K	L	M	N	O	P	Q	R	S	T	U	V	W	X	Y	Z
B	B	C	D	E	F	G	H	I	J	K	L	M	N	O	P	Q	R	S	T	U	V	W	X	Y	Z	A
C	C	D	E	F	G	H	I	J	K	L	M	N	O	P	Q	R	S	T	U	V	W	X	Y	Z	A	B
D	D	E	F	G	H	I	J	K	L	M	N	O	P	Q	R	S	T	U	V	W	X	Y	Z	A	B	C
E	E	F	G	H	I	J	K	L	M	N	O	P	Q	R	S	T	U	V	W	X	Y	Z	A	B	C	D
F	F	G	H	I	J	K	L	M	N	O	P	Q	R	S	T	U	V	W	X	Y	Z	A	B	C	D	E
G	G	H	I	J	K	L	M	N	O	P	Q	R	S	T	U	V	W	X	Y	Z	A	B	C	D	E	F
H	H	I	J	K	L	M	N	O	P	Q	R	S	T	U	V	W	X	Y	Z	A	B	C	D	E	F	G
I	I	J	K	L	M	N	O	P	Q	R	S	T	U	V	W	X	Y	Z	A	B	C	D	E	F	G	H
J	J	K	L	M	N	O	P	Q	R	S	T	U	V	W	X	Y	Z	A	B	C	D	E	F	G	H	I
K	K	L	M	N	O	P	Q	R	S	T	U	V	W	X	Y	Z	A	B	C	D	E	F	G	H	I	J
L	L	M	N	O	P	Q	R	S	T	U	V	W	X	Y	Z	A	B	C	D	E	F	G	H	I	J	K
M	M	N	O	P	Q	R	S	T	U	V	W	X	Y	Z	A	B	C	D	E	F	G	H	I	J	K	L
N	N	O	P	Q	R	S	T	U	V	W	X	Y	Z	A	B	C	D	E	F	G	H	I	J	K	L	M
O	O	P	Q	R	S	T	U	V	W	X	Y	Z	A	B	C	D	E	F	G	H	I	J	K	L	M	N
P	P	Q	R	S	T	U	V	W	X	Y	Z	A	B	C	D	E	F	G	H	I	J	K	L	M	N	O
Q	Q	R	S	T	U	V	W	X	Y	Z	A	B	C	D	E	F	G	H	I	J	K	L	M	N	O	P
R	R	S	T	U	V	W	X	Y	Z	A	B	C	D	E	F	G	H	I	J	K	L	M	N	O	P	Q
S	S	T	U	V	W	X	Y	Z	A	B	C	D	E	F	G	H	I	J	K	L	M	N	O	P	Q	R
T	T	U	V	W	X	Y	Z	A	B	C	D	E	F	G	H	I	J	K	L	M	N	O	P	Q	R	S
U	U	V	W	X	Y	Z	A	B	C	D	E	F	G	H	I	J	K	L	M	N	O	P	Q	R	S	T
V	V	W	X	Y	Z	A	B	C	D	E	F	G	H	I	J	K	L	M	N	O	P	Q	R	S	T	U
W	W	X	Y	Z	A	B	C	D	E	F	G	H	I	J	K	L	M	N	O	P	Q	R	S	T	U	V
X	X	Y	Z	A	B	C	D	E	F	G	H	I	J	K	L	M	N	O	P	Q	R	S	T	U	V	W
Y	Y	Z	A	B	C	D	E	F	G	H	I	J	K	L	M	N	O	P	Q	R	S	T	U	V	W	X
Z	Z	A	B	C	D	E	F	G	H	I	J	K	L	M	N	O	P	Q	R	S	T	U	V	W	X	Y

Decode a Vigenère

Many ciphers require working backward to reveal messages. The Vigenère cipher does, too. Try to decode the ciphertext YYIXGFXKVRCTNJHBWIQVXEQBGCI using the keystream *french*. (Note: If you use the tabula recta above, ignore the color-coding!)

33

Cipher Machines

Computers now help us create sophisticated ciphers, but long ago, people had to rely on their wits alone to devise new and clever methods of making cryptographs. Eventually, this led to the invention of simple devices that could generate complicated ciphers. Encryption devices first appeared around 400 BC. Over time, they evolved into complex machines, challenging even the most-skilled codebreakers.

Spartan Encryption

One of the first transposition cipher devices was the Spartan **scytale** (SKIH-tuh-lee). To make the scytale, the encoder used a wooden rod and a long strip of leather. The encoder first attached the leather to one end of the rod. The next step was to wrap the leather strip around and around so there was no overlap. Finally, he or she could write the message in a straight line on the wound leather across the length of the rod. After unwinding the strip, the letters appeared randomly placed and seemingly meaningless. To read the message, the receiver needed an identical rod to wrap the letter strip around to reveal the message.

Spartan Belts

After creating the cipher using the scytale, a **courier** could wear the strip like a belt. As long as the message was facing inwards, the concealed cipher was out of sight and ready for a long journey before reaching the destination.

The Enigma

The **infamous** Enigma machine was used by the German military in World War II. It used sets of rotating disks to mechanically compute ciphertext. It was capable of making nearly 159 quintillion different combinations. (That's 159 with 18 zeros after it!) The user first typed a message on the lower set of keys. Each time the user would push a letter, the rotors would turn, and the equivalent ciphertext letter would light up in the upper section. The user would then send the ciphertext in a written message or over a telegraph in Morse code.

The Germans sent new key settings each day. This meant that even if the Allies broke a coded message, the key settings would change before they could crack future messages. The Germans thought the Enigma was unbreakable. But with the help of a Polish codebreaking machine called the Bombe, codebreakers were finally able to crack the Enigma.

Bletchley Park

During World War II, the British established a codebreaking facility at Bletchley Park, an estate in England. They employed the brightest people of the day. The codebreakers intercepted many German communications. Using the Bombe, they gained valuable information that gave the Allies an advantage over Germany.

the Enigma

Modern Cryptography

From the birth of cryptography in ancient Egypt until the 1970s, the only way to encrypt anything was with symmetric cryptography. This is when both the sender and the receiver need the same key to encrypt or decrypt a secret message. But modern cryptography is built on asymmetric cryptography. That means there are two keys—the key used to encrypt a message cannot be used to decrypt the message. One key is made public. The other is kept a secret. This type of cryptography is the most widespread and secure method used today.

Alice, Bob, and Eve

Rather than using abstract characters to describe a scenario, such as "Party A" or "Party B," relatable terms make it much easier to follow. Widely used within the field of cryptography, "Alice" typically represents the message sender, "Bob" represents the message receiver, and "Eve" represents the eavesdropper, the person trying to intercept the message.

Party A

Twenty-First-Century Concerns

Why are more secure codes needed today? Pretend Alice wants to send Bob a secret message over the Internet. Now, picture someone named Eve, who is an "eavesdropper," waiting for the right time to intercept the message and steal Alice and Bob's secret. Encryption today focuses on the Eves of the world, who lurk on websites, in email viruses, and in so many other virtual places. The goal is to keep the key out of Eve's hands and protect valuable virtual data.

The concerns of today echo the same concerns from ancient times, but now interception can occur from halfway around the world in a matter of seconds. With electronics, computers, and the Internet as central parts of daily life, people now need more secure methods of communicating secrets virtually.

Eavesdropper

Party B

An Asymmetric Story

To better understand asymmetric encryption, consider the following analogy:

Picture an open padlock; anybody is capable of picking it up and shutting it. But only the owner of the padlock has the key to unlock it. Our friend Bob has a bunch of open padlocks available for anybody to use so they can send Bob messages. All the locks open with the same key, but nobody has the key except Bob. So when Alice wants to send Bob a message, Alice borrows one of Bob's open padlocks, inserts the message, and locks it up securely. The locked message is then sent to Bob, and only Bob can use the key to unlock, decrypt, and read it.

There's a lot of mathematics involved in this type of encryption. Its process is completed using prime numbers and a very complicated algorithm. Prime numbers are used because there are no patterns or algorithms that can easily predict prime numbers.

Codebreaking Computers

Computers make it easier to crack codes and ciphers. In fact, processing power doubles every couple of years. If your cipher takes one year to break today, people may not even attempt to break it. But computers built nine years from now may be able to crack that same code in less than six days.

Into the Future

Cryptography has shaped the history of the world, from kings and queens in **antiquity** to the average person today. And we have to wonder: What would have happened if someone intercepted secret messages about the plan to assassinate President Lincoln? What might the world be like if the Allies had never cracked the Enigma during World War II? What might have been the outcome of the war without the help of code users?

Cryptography is a mighty tool that can be used for good *and* for bad. The techniques to encode messages have evolved over time, but the goals remain the same. Cryptographers strive to protect top-secret information from interception. They also need to intercept messages to prevent tragedies, such as wars and terrorism.

For the average person, cryptography remains behind the scenes. It's intertwined in the everyday tasks people complete online, on cell phones, and on other devices. But it is always there, thanks to the scholars and codebreakers who worked through the centuries to turn cryptography into what it is today.

Future Codebreakers

Did you love solving the ciphers in this book? Does the thought of intercepting confidential military and government information excite you? You might have what it takes to become a professional cryptanalyst for the National Security Agency, the Central Intelligence Agency, or other security and research agencies.

This is a codebreaking digital computer developed during WWII.

Glossary

advent—the coming into use

antiquity—ancient times

ciphers—scrambled messages created with the use of algorithms or step-by-step procedures that perform encryptions or decryptions

courier—a person who delivers packages and messages

cover text—the text, image, or audio used to conceal a secret message, used in regards to steganography

cryptanalysts—people who study ciphers, ciphertext, or cryptography

cryptographer—a person who writes in codes or ciphers

cryptographs—messages written in codes or ciphers

declassified—information that was previously held secret by the government but later made public

decrypted—changed a ciphertext into plaintext

encryption—to convert a message into a code

Freemasons—members of a worldwide secret fraternity that promotes brotherly love and support for its members

infamous—well known for negative reasons

interception—seizing control of a correspondence that was intended for someone else

key—the tool needed to encrypt or decrypt a message

keystream—random characters or a recognizable word that when used with plaintext, helps produce polyalphabetic ciphertext

keyword—a word that helps decode a cipher

null—a placeholder representation of an empty value

persecution—hostility toward a group of people or a person due to race, political, or religious beliefs

polyalphabetic—made using multiple alphabets to encrypt a correspondence

scytale—cylindrical tool with strips of parchment or leather wound around it to transpose a cipher

steganography—the study of concealing a message within an otherwise ordinary correspondence

stegotext—an encrypted message hidden within cover text

Index

Check It Out!

Books

Blackwood, Gary. 2009. *Mysterious Messages: A History of Codes and Ciphers*. Dutton Children's Books.

Bruchac, Joseph. 2006. *Code Talker: A Novel About the Navajo Marines of World War Two*. Speak.

Gilbert, Adrian. 2009. *Codes and Ciphers*. Firefly Books Ltd.

Lunde, Paul. 2009. *The Book of Codes: Understanding the World of Hidden Messages: An Illustrated Guide to Signs, Symbols, Ciphers, and Secret Languages*. University of California Press.

Singh, Simon. 1999. *The Code Book: The Evolution of Secrecy from Mary, Queen of Scots to Quantum Cryptography*. Doubleday.

Video

Day, Philip, and David C. Taylor. *Great Escape: The Final Secrets*. National Geographic Channel.

Websites

British Broadcasting Corporation. *Enigma*. http://www.bbc.co.uk/history/topics/enigma.

CryptoClub Team. *Crypto Club*. http://www.cryptoclub.org/.

National Security Agency. *CryptoKids® America's Future Codemakers & Codebreakers*. https://www.nsa.gov/kids/home_html.shtml.

Try It!

Imagine that you are a spy and you need to send an encrypted message to your friends and family. You only have a small piece of paper with room for a five-line message—anything bigger than that may be discovered in transit. To do this, you must create a written means of communicating that would not be easily deciphered. Before writing the message, you have some work to do:

- Plan your coding system. What symbols will represent the letters of the alphabet? Will your code have numbers or punctuation marks in it? If so, what symbols will represent each digit and mark?

- Decide your means of communicating. Are you going to write in complete sentences? Will you use "text talk" or sentence fragments?

- Decide what your message will say. Are you writing for help? Do you need to describe where you are? Or are you explaining your journey?

- Then, encrypt your message. Give it to a friend, and see if he or she can decipher it.

About the Author

Rane Anderson lives in Colorado with her husband and son. She earned a bachelor of science in geology from California State University, Long Beach. When she's not writing or scaling mountains, she's trying to solve an even greater mystery than codes and ciphers: how to get her toddler to eat his vegetables!

Answers

page 19—Cipher Blast!: *The ballot is stronger than the bullet*; a quote from Abraham Lincoln

page 20—Route Cipher: 2 columns x 18 rows, 3 columns x 12 rows, 4 columns x 9 rows, or 6 columns by 6 rows

page 24—Caesar's Simple Cipher: three

page 26—Thinking Like a Codebreaker: *We are awesome.*

page 29—Pigpen Cipher: *rail fence cipher three row key*

page 33—Decode a Vigenère: *the keystream is double trouble*

page 27—The Ultimate Challenge: The first provided clue was *double trouble*. On the next page, there is a paragraph titled "Double Trouble." This paragraph is about double encryptions. It reads, "For example, try using the Vigenère cipher and then transposing that ciphertext with a rail fence cipher." This tells us to decode the Ultimate Challenge message first using a Vigenère and then a rail fence cipher. Then, solving the pigpen cipher on page 29 tells us that the rail fence cipher uses a three-row key. Lastly, the Vigenère cipher on page 33 tells us the keystream is *double trouble*. Decode ECFHXXKMQUMYIRDYFLLXTZ using the Vigenère with this keystream. That gives the new ciphertext: BOLGMTRVCALNEOPEEAHECL. Lastly, use the rail fence cipher with a three-row key to get the plaintext answer: *Bravo, challenge complete!*